M000158835

BELIEVE IN YOURSELF.

summersdale

BELIEVE IN YOURSELF

An Hachette UK Company
www.hachette.co.uk

Summersdale Publishers Ltd
Part of Octopus Publishing Group Limited
Carmelite House
50 Victoria Embankment
LONDON
EC4Y 0DZ
UK

www.summersdale.com

Printed and bound in Poland

ISBN: 978-1-78685-960-0

Substantial discounts on bulk quantities of Summersdale books are available to corporations, professional associations and other organizations. For details contact general enquiries: telephone: +44 (0) 1243 771107 or email: enquiries@summersdale.com.

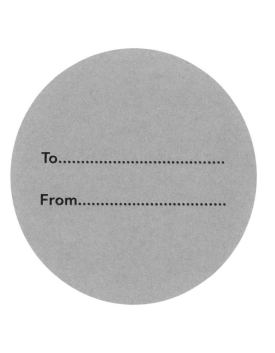

To.....................................

From.....................................

As soon as you
trust yourself,
you will know
how to live.

Johann Wolfgang von Goethe

I just breathe
and believe.

Jodi Livon

You are magnificent
beyond measure, perfect
in your imperfections,
and wonderfully made.

Abiola Abrams

YOU HAVE TO BE ABLE TO LOVE YOURSELF BECAUSE THAT'S WHEN THINGS FALL INTO PLACE.

Vanessa Hudgens

Never dull your shine
for somebody else.

Tyra Banks

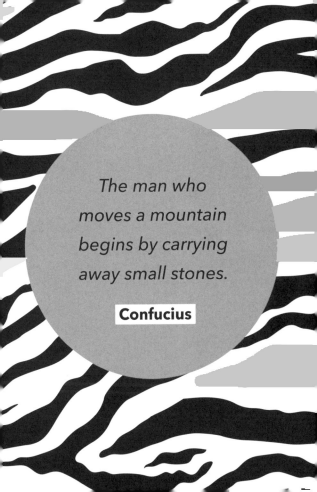

The man who moves a mountain begins by carrying away small stones.

Confucius

You are never too old
to set another goal or
to dream a new dream.

Les Brown

Doubt whom you will,
but never yourself.

Christian Nestell Bovee

LEARN TO LAUGH IN THE FACE OF FEAR.

The way you carry yourself is influenced by the way you feel inside.

Marilyn Monroe

WE BECOME WHAT WE THINK ABOUT.

Earl Nightingale

If you really want
something, you can
figure out how to
make it happen.

Cher

What you do today
can improve all
your tomorrows.

Ralph Marston

You only get one chance at life and you have to grab it boldly.

Bear Grylls

The more we do, the
more we can do.

William Hazlitt

IT IS CONFIDENCE
IN OUR BODIES,
MINDS AND
SPIRITS THAT
ALLOWS US TO
KEEP LOOKING
FOR NEW
ADVENTURES.

Oprah Winfrey

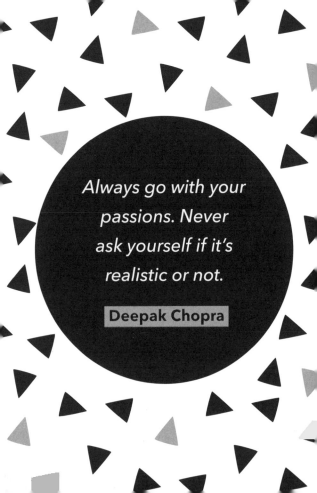

Always go with your passions. Never ask yourself if it's realistic or not.

Deepak Chopra

IT IS NOT THE MOUNTAINS WE CONQUER, BUT OURSELVES.

Edmund Hillary

FEEL
GOOD

IN THE SKIN YOU'RE IN.

Act the way you
want to feel.

Gretchen Rubin

Sometimes the smallest step in the right direction ends up being the biggest step of your life.

Naeem Callaway

Nothing can dim the light which shines from within.

Maya Angelou

When you reach the
end of your rope,
tie a knot in it
and hang on.

American proverb

THE QUESTION ISN'T WHO IS GOING TO LET ME; IT'S WHO IS GOING TO STOP ME.

Ayn Rand

I am only one, but I am one. I can't do everything, but I can do something. The something I ought to do, I can do.

Edward Everett Hale

Speak up, believe in yourself, take risks.

Sheryl Sandberg

FAITH IS TAKING THE FIRST STEP, EVEN WHEN YOU DON'T SEE THE WHOLE STAIRCASE.

Martin Luther King Jr

No one can make you feel inferior without your consent.

Eleanor Roosevelt

I am the master
of my fate: I am the
captain of my soul.

William Ernest Henley

FIND A WAY, NOT AN EXCUSE.

Don't waste your energy
trying to educate or
change opinions...
Do your thing and don't
care if they like it.

Tina Fey

CONSTANT REPETITION CARRIES CONVICTION.

Robert Collier

*Fear is only
as deep as the
mind allows.*

Japanese proverb

Hide not your talents,
they for use were made.
What's a sundial
in the shade?

Benjamin Franklin

Look up, laugh
loud, talk big, keep
the colour in your
cheek and the
fire in your eye.

William Hazlitt

OPTIMISM IS THE FAITH THAT LEADS TO ACHIEVEMENT; NOTHING CAN BE DONE WITHOUT HOPE.

Helen Keller

Self-trust is the first
secret to success.

Ralph Waldo Emerson

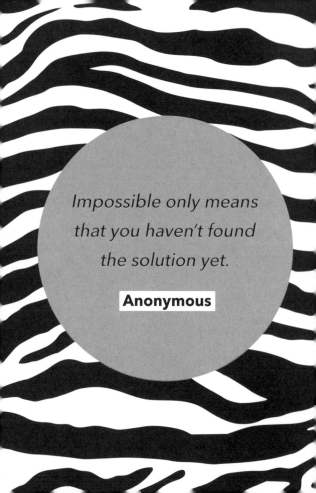

Impossible only means that you haven't found the solution yet.

Anonymous

No one except you
alone can change
your life.

M. K. Soni

We have to dare to
be ourselves, however
frightening or strange
that self may prove to be.

May Sarton

Never give up then,
for that's just the
place and time that
the tide'll turn.

Harriet Beecher Stowe

YOU CAN ACHIEVE WHATEVER YOU WANT.

There was never a
night or a problem
that could defeat
sunrise or hope.

Bernard Williams

OPPORTUNITIES MULTIPLY AS THEY ARE SEIZED.

Sun Tzu

Most of the important things in the world have been accomplished by people who have kept on trying when there seemed to be no hope at all.

Dale Carnegie

It's not whether
you get knocked
down. It's whether
you get up again.

Vince Lombardi

Life shrinks or expands according to one's courage.

Anaïs Nin

It is not because things
are difficult that we do
not dare; it is because
we do not dare that
they are difficult.

Seneca

OPTIMISM IS THE ONE QUALITY MORE ASSOCIATED WITH SUCCESS AND HAPPINESS THAN ANY OTHER.

Brian Tracy

First say to yourself who you would be; and then do what you have to do.

Epictetus

People may doubt
what you say, but
they will believe
what you do.

Lewis Cass

THE
HIGHER
YOU JUMP,

THE
CLOSER
YOU GET.

To live a creative life,
we must lose our fear
of being wrong.

Joseph Chilton Pearce

Be sure what you want
and be sure about
yourself... You have
to believe in yourself
and be strong.

Adriana Lima

Put your future in good hands – your own.

Mark Victor Hansen

Your past is not
your potential.

Marilyn Ferguson

BELIEVE IN YOURSELF! HAVE FAITH IN YOUR ABILITIES!

Norman Vincent Peale

I'M NOT GOING TO LIMIT MYSELF JUST BECAUSE PEOPLE WON'T ACCEPT THE FACT THAT I CAN DO SOMETHING ELSE.

Dolly Parton

THROW CAUTION TO THE WIND AND JUST DO IT.

Niamh Greene

Success is a science;
if you have the conditions,
you get the result.

Oscar Wilde

Freedom lies in
being bold.

Robert Frost

We must not
allow other people's
limited perceptions
to define us.

Virginia Satir

NEVER
EVER
GIVE UP.

There's nothing more
intoxicating than doing
big, bold things.

Jason Kilar

Scared is what you're feeling… brave is what you're doing.

Emma Donoghue

DON'T WAIT. THE TIME WILL NEVER BE JUST RIGHT.

Napoleon Hill

You defeat defeatism
with confidence.

Vince Lombardi

I shall either
find a way or
make one.

Hannibal

We always may
be what we might
have been.

Adelaide Anne Procter

Out of difficulties
grow miracles.

Jean de La Bruyère

INSIDE EVERY HUMAN BEING THERE ARE TREASURES TO UNLOCK.

Mike Huckabee

The best preparation
for tomorrow is doing
your best today.

H. Jackson Brown Jr

LIVE LIFE TO THE FULLEST, AND FOCUS ON THE POSITIVE.

Matt Cameron

Very little is needed to make a happy life. It is all within yourself, in your way of thinking.

Marcus Aurelius

BELIEVE YOU CAN AND YOU WILL!

The secret of getting ahead is getting started.

Anonymous

Destiny is not
a matter of chance;
it is a matter of choice.
It is not a thing to be
waited for; it is a thing
to be achieved.

William Jennings Bryan

OPPORTUNITIES DON'T HAPPEN; YOU CREATE THEM.

Chris Grosser

To accomplish
great things, we must
not only act, but also
dream; not only plan,
but also believe.

Anatole France

The most difficult thing is the decision to act. The rest is merely tenacity.

Amelia Earhart

It is the same with people as it is with riding a bike. Only when moving can one comfortably maintain one's balance.

Albert Einstein

EVERYTHING YOU'VE EVER WANTED IS ON THE OTHER SIDE OF FEAR.

George Addair

You just can't beat the person who never gives up.

Babe Ruth

So many of our dreams at first seem impossible, then they seem improbable, and then, when we summon the will, they soon become inevitable.

Christopher Reeve

LET
YOUR
FAITH
BE

BIGGER
THAN
YOUR
FEARS.

There will be obstacles.
There will be doubters.
There will be mistakes.
But with hard work...
there are no limits.

Michael Phelps

A happy person is not a person in a certain set of circumstances, but rather a person with a certain set of attitudes.

Hugh Downs

Every artist was first an amateur.

Ralph Waldo Emerson

With confidence, you
have won even before
you have started.

Marcus Garvey

How many things are looked upon as quite impossible, until they have been actually effected?

Pliny the Elder

Nothing in life is to
be feared; it is only
to be understood.

Marie Curie

**DON'T LOAF
AND INVITE
INSPIRATION;
LIGHT OUT AFTER
IT WITH A CLUB.**

Jack London

Character is destiny.

Heraclitus

You need to be so sure about yourself and your ideas that your confidence convinces others too.

Rami Shaar

THE SELF IS NOT SOMETHING THAT ONE FINDS. IT IS SOMETHING ONE CREATES.

Thomas Szasz

MISTAKES ARE PROOF THAT YOU'RE TRYING.

To achieve greatness
start where you are,
use what you have,
and do what you can.

Arthur Ashe

Believe that life *is* worth living and your belief will help create the fact.

William James

Courage is found
in unlikely places.

J. R. R. Tolkien

Know that you are
not stuck where you
are unless you
decide to be.

Wayne W. Dyer

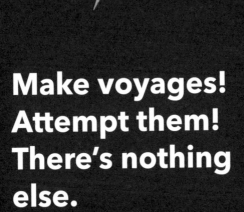

Make voyages! Attempt them! There's nothing else.

Tennessee Williams

You've got to seize
the opportunity if it is
presented to you.

Clive Davis

Accept the challenges
so that you may feel the
exhilaration of victory.

George S. Patton

YOU'VE GOT TO GET UP EVERY MORNING WITH DETERMINATION IF YOU'RE GOING TO GO TO BED WITH SATISFACTION.

George Lorimer

Courage doesn't always roar. Sometimes courage is the quiet voice at the end of the day, saying, "I will try again tomorrow."

Mary Anne Radmacher

You can never leave
footprints that last
if you are always
walking on tiptoe.

Leymah Gbowee

HOPE IS THE KEY TO HAPPINESS, WHICH IS THE KEY TO SUCCESS.

Herman Cain

**THE FUTURE
IS YOURS
TO CREATE.**

I believe in myself,
even my most delicate
intangible feelings.

Marilyn Monroe

A lot of people are afraid
to say what they want.
That's why they don't
get what they want.

Madonna

Either you run the day
or the day runs you.

Jim Rohn

Our greatest fear as individuals... should not be of failure but of succeeding at things in life that don't really matter.

Tim Kizziar

If I am not for myself,

who will be for me?

Hillel

GOOD THINGS COME TO PEOPLE WHO WAIT, BUT BETTER THINGS COME TO THOSE WHO GO OUT AND GET THEM.

Anonymous

If you don't like
something, change it;
if you can't change it,
change the way you
think about it.

Mary Engelbreit

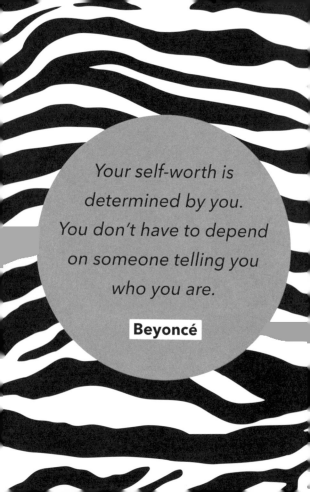

Your self-worth is determined by you. You don't have to depend on someone telling you who you are.

Beyoncé

Real difficulties can be overcome. It is only the imaginary ones that are unconquerable.

Theodore N. Vail

NEVER THINK YOU AREN'T WORTHY ENOUGH –

YOU ARE.

The future belongs to those who have the courage to believe in the beauty of their dreams.

Anonymous

Our greatest glory
is not in never falling,
but in rising every
time we fall.

Oliver Goldsmith

We know what
we are, but
know not what
we may be.

William Shakespeare

Belief in oneself is one of the most important bricks in building any successful venture.

Lydia Maria Child

YOUR PRESENT CIRCUMSTANCES DON'T DETERMINE WHERE YOU CAN GO; THEY MERELY DETERMINE WHERE YOU START.

Nido Qubein

It takes courage to
grow up and become
who you really are.

E. E. Cummings

People may *hear*
your words, but they
feel your attitude.

John C. Maxwell

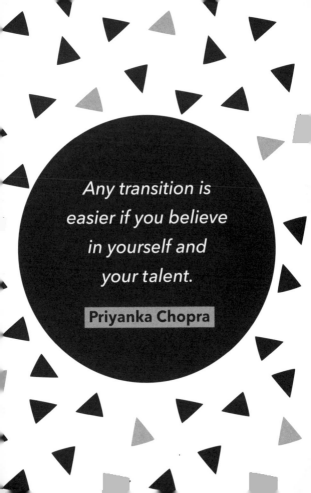

Any transition is easier if you believe in yourself and your talent.

Priyanka Chopra

UNFOLD YOUR
OWN MYTH.

Rumi

Success is a state
of mind. If you want
success, start thinking
of yourself as a success.

Joyce Brothers

NOTHING IS IMPOSSIBLE.

Whether you
believe you can
do a thing or not,
you are right.

Henry Ford

Be yourself. An original is always worth more than a copy.

Suzy Kassem

SUCCESS USUALLY COMES TO THOSE WHO ARE TOO BUSY TO BE LOOKING FOR IT.

Henry David Thoreau

When you own the story, you get to write the ending!

Brené Brown

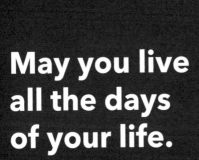

**May you live
all the days
of your life.**

Jonathan Swift

Just as much as we see in others, we have in ourselves.

William Hazlitt

Turn your wounds
into wisdom.

Oprah Winfrey

Someone's opinion of you does not have to become your reality.

Les Brown

DO NOT FORGET YOUR DUTY TO LOVE YOURSELF.

Søren Kierkegaard

You can be the ripest, juiciest peach in the world, and there's still going to be somebody who hates peaches.

Dita Von Teese

In the depths of winter,
I finally learned that
within me there lay an
invincible summer.

Albert Camus

FOLLOW YOUR DREAMS, WHEREVER THEY TAKE YOU.

I can be changed by
what happens to me.
But I refuse to be
reduced by it.

Maya Angelou

It's kind of fun
to do the
impossible.

Walt Disney

YOU WERE BORN WITH WINGS. WHY PREFER TO CRAWL THROUGH LIFE?

Rumi

A ship is safe
in harbour, but
that's not what
ships are for.

John A. Shedd

The past has no power over the present moment.

Eckhart Tolle

I owe my success to having listened respectfully and rather bashfully to the very best advice… and then going away and doing the exact opposite.

G. K. Chesterton

TO SHINE YOUR BRIGHTEST LIGHT IS TO BE WHO YOU TRULY ARE.

Roy T. Bennett

YOU YOURSELF, AS
MUCH AS ANYBODY
IN THE ENTIRE
UNIVERSE, DESERVE
YOUR LOVE AND
AFFECTION.

Anonymous

It is better to fail in originality, than to succeed in imitation.

Herman Melville

IF YOU
BELIEVE

THEN
YOU WILL
ACHIEVE.

If you're interested in finding out more about our books, find us on Facebook at **Summersdale Publishers** and follow us on Twitter at **@Summersdale**.

www.summersdale.com

Image credits

Lightning bolt on pp.4, 39, 73, 107, 141
© Shutterstock.com

Zebra print pattern on pp.9, 42, 88, 122
© yellowpixel/Shutterstock.com

Triangles pattern on pp.20, 54, 133
© Alex Landa/Shutterstock.com

Star icon on pp.26, 60, 94, 128, 160
© Alex Kednert/Shutterstock.com

Snowflake pattern on pp.31, 76, 110, 156
© Oxy_gen/Shutterstock.com

Fist icon on pp.17, 51, 85, 119, 153
© Brian Goff/Shutterstock.com